Personal Financial Planner

for use with

Personal Finance

Sixth Edition

Jack Kapoor
College of DuPage

Les Dlabay
Lake Forest College

Robert Hughes
Dallas County Community College

Prepared by
Les Dlabay
Lake Forest College

Boston   Burr Ridge, IL   Dubuque, IA   Madison, WI   New York   San Francisco   St. Louis
Bangkok   Bogotá   Caracas   Lisbon   London   Madrid
Mexico City   Milan   New Delhi   Seoul   Singapore   Sydney   Taipei   Toronto

Personal Financial Planner for use with
PERSONAL FINANCE (SIXTH EDITION)
Jack Kapoor, Les Dlabay, Robert Hughes

Published by Irwin/McGraw-Hill, an imprint of the McGraw-Hill Companies, Inc., 1221 Avenue of the Americas, New York, NY 10020. Copyright © 2001, 1999, 1996, 1994, 1991 by the McGraw-Hill Companies, Inc. All rights reserved.

1 2 3 4 5 6 7 8 9 0 QPD/QPD 0 9 8 7 6 5 4 3 2 1 0

ISBN 0-07-238073-X

Personal Financial Planner

Preface

This *Personal Financial Planner* is packaged free with each copy of *Personal Finance*, Sixth Edition, by Kapoor, Dlabay, and Hughes purchased from McGraw-Hill Companies. This resource booklet is designed to help you create and implement a personal financial plan. The worksheets in this *Personal Financial Planner* are divided into the following main sections:

A – Personal Data and Goals
B – Career Planning
C – Money Management and Budgeting
D – Tax Planning
E – Banking Services
F – Consumer Credit
G – Consumer Buying
H – Housing
I – Insurance
J – Investments
K – Retirement and Estate Planning
L – Financial Plan Summary

Items to consider when using this Personal Financial Planner

1. Since this publication is designed to adapt to every personal financial situation, some of the sheets may be appropriate for you at this time, and not at other times in your life.

2. Each of the sheets in the first 11 sections is referenced to specific page numbers of *Personal Finance*, Sixth Edition, to help you better understand a topic. In addition, each sheet has one of the following symbols to highlight if it should be used in the planning, research, or summary phase of your financial decision making:

 **Planning Sheet**

 **Research Sheet**

 **Summary Sheet**

3.   Some sheets may need to be used more than once (such as preparing a personal cash flow statement or a budget). You are encouraged to photocopy additional sheets as needed.

4.   To assist you with using the internet for financial planning information, Web sites are listed on the opening page of each section.

5.   Finally, remember personal financial planning is an ongoing activity. With the use of this booklet, the textbook, and your efforts, an organized and satisfying personal economic existence can be yours.

Note: The sheets in this booklet along with other financial planning calculation tools, are available on the Windows® version of *Personal Finance*, Sixth Edition, CD-ROM.

Personal Financial Planner

Table of Contents

Section A

Personal data and goals

The worksheets in this section are to be used with Chapter 1 of *Personal Finance*, Sixth Edition.

Sheet 1   Personal information sheet

Sheet 2   Financial institutions and advisors

Sheet 3   Goal setting sheet

Sheet 4   Monitoring current economic conditions

Sheet 5   Time value of money calculations

Web sites for Financial Planning

Standard & Poors personal finance site	www.personalwealth.com
FinanCenter	www.financecenter.com
Money Central	www.moneycentral.msn.com
Motley Fool	www.fool.com
CNN Financial News	www.cnnfn.com/index.html
Quicken	www.qfn.com
U.S. Federal Reserve System	www.federalreserve.gov
Consumer Price Index & inflation data	www.bls.gov
	www.stls.frb.org/fred/data/cupdate.html
Calculators for the time-value of money	www.centura.com/formulas/calc.html
	www.moneyadvisor.com/calc
Money Magazine	www.money.com
Kiplinger's Personal Finance Magazine	www.kiplinger.com
Business Week Magazine	www.businessweek.com
Worth Magazine	www.worth.com
Smart Money Magazine	www.smartmoney.com
The Wall Street Journal	www.wsj.com

Sheet 1 – Personal information sheet

Purpose: To provide quick reference for vital household data.
Instructions: Provide the personal and financial data requested below.

For use with
Personal Finance
Sixth Ed., Kapoor,
Dlabay & Hughes
Page 4

Name _____ _____

Birthdate _____ _____

Marital Status _____ _____

Address _____ _____

Phone _____ _____

e-mail _____ _____

Social Security No. _____ _____

Drivers License No. _____ _____

Place of Employment _____ _____

Address _____ _____

Phone _____ _____

Position _____ _____

Length of Service _____ _____

Checking Acct. No. _____ _____

Financial Inst. _____ _____

Address _____ _____

Phone _____ _____

Dependent data

Name	Birthdate	Relationship	Social Security No.
_____	_____	_____	_____
_____	_____	_____	_____
_____	_____	_____	_____
_____	_____	_____	_____

Sheet 2 – Financial institutions and advisors

Purpose: To create a directory of commonly used financial institutions and financial planning professionals.

Instructions: Provide the information in the spaces proved.

For use with
Personal Finance
Sixth Ed., Kapoor,
Dlabay & Hughes
Page 4

Attorney
Name _____
Address _____
_____
Phone _____
Fax _____
e-mail _____

Primary financial institution
Name _____
Address _____
_____
Phone _____
Fax _____
Checking
Acct. No. _____
Savings
Acct. No. _____
Loan No. _____

Insurance (home/auto
Agent _____
Company _____
Address _____
_____
Phone _____
Fax _____
Policy No. _____
e-mail _____

Credit card 1
Issuer _____
Address _____
_____
Phone _____
Fax _____
Acct. No. _____
Exp. Date _____
Limit _____

Credit card 2
Issuer _____
Address _____
_____
Phone _____
Fax _____
Acct. No. _____
Exp. Date _____
Limit _____

Tax preparer
Name _____
Firm _____
Address _____
_____
Phone _____
Fax _____
e-mail _____

(continued)

Sheet 2 (continued)

Insurance (life/health)

Agent _____

Company _____

Address _____

_____

Phone _____

Fax _____

e-mail _____

Policy No. _____

Real estate agent

Name _____

Company _____

Address _____

_____

Phone _____

Fax _____

e-mail _____

Investment broker

Name _____

Address _____

_____

Phone _____

Fax _____

e-mail _____

Acct. No. _____

Investment company

Name _____

Address _____

_____

Phone _____

Fax _____

Acct. No. _____

e-mail _____

Web site _____

Sheet 3 - Goal setting sheet

Purpose: To identify personal financial goals and create an action plan.

Instructions: Based on personal and household needs and values, identify specific goals that require action.

For use with
Personal Finance
Sixth Ed., Kapoor,
Dlabay & Hughes
Pages 10–12

Short-term monetary goals (less than two years)

Description	Amount needed	Months to achieve	Action to be taken	Priority
Example: pay off credit card debt	$850	12	Use money from pay raise	High

Intermediate and long-term monetary goals

Description	Amount needed	Months to achieve	Action to be taken	Priority

Non-monetary goals

Description	Time frame	Actions to be taken
Example: set up file for personal financial records and documents	next 2-3 months	locate all personal and financial records and documents; set up files for various spending, saving, borrowing categories

Sheet 4 - Monitoring current economic conditions

Purpose: To monitor selected economic indicators that influence various saving, investing, spending, and borrowing decisions.
Instructions: Using *The Wall Street Journal*, World Wide Web, or other sources of economic information, obtain current data for various economic factors.

For use with
Personal Finance
Sixth Ed., Kapoor,
Dlabay & Hughes
Pages 13–16

Economic Factor	Recent trends	Possible influences on financial planning decisions
Example: Mortgage rates	decline in mortgage rates	consider buying a home; consider refinancing an existing mortgage
Interest rates		
Consumer prices		
Other: _____		
Other: _____		
Other: _____		

Sheet 5 – Time value of money calculations

Purpose: To calculate future and present value amounts related to financial planning decisions.

Instructions: Use a calculator or future or present value tables to compute the time value of money.

For use with
Personal Finance
Sixth Ed., Kapoor,
Dlabay & Hughes
Pages 17–20

Future value of a single amount

- to determine future value of a single amount
- to determine interest lost when cash purchase is made

(Use Exhibit A-1 in Appendix A)

current amount	times	future value factor	equals	future value amount
$_____	x	$_____	=	$_____

Future value of a series of deposits

- to determine future values of regular savings deposits
- to determine future value of regular retirement deposits

(Use Exhibit A-2 in Appendix A)

regular deposit amount	times	future value of annuity factor	equals	future value amount
$_____	x	$_____	=	$_____

Present value of a single amount

- to determine an amount to be deposited now that will grow to desired amount

(Use Exhibit A-3 in Appendix A)

future amount desired	times	present value factor	equals	present value amount
$_____	x	$_____	=	$_____

Present value of a series of deposits

- to determine an amount that can be withdrawn on a regular basis

(Use Exhibit A-4 in Appendix A)

regular amount to be withdrawn	times	present value of annuity factor	equals	present value amount
$_____	x	$_____	=	$_____

Section B

Career planning

The worksheets in this section are used with Chapter 2 of *Personal Finance*, Sixth Edition.

Web sites for Career Planning

Career planning tips	www.jobtrak.com.
	www.careers.wsj.com
	www.careermag.com
	www.mapping-your-future.org
Listings of available jobs	www.careermosaic.com
	www.careerpath.com
	www.hotjobs.com
	www.careerbuilder.com
	www.monster.com
Résumé preparation advice	www.occ.com
	www.jobweb.com
U.S. Dept. of Labor & state agencies	www.ajb.dni.us

Sheet 6 – Career area research sheet

Purpose: To become familiar with work activities and career requirements for a field of employment.

Instructions: Using the *Career Occupational Outlook Handbook* and other information sources (library materials, interviews), obtain information related to one or more career areas of interest to you.

For use with
Personal Finance
Sixth Ed., Kapoor,
Dlabay & Hughes
Pages 39, 40

Career area/job title		
Nature of the work general activities and duties		
Working conditions physical surroundings, hours, mental and physical demands		
Training and other qualifications		
Job outlook future prospect for employment in this field		
Earnings starting and advanced		
Additional information		
Other questions that require further research		
Sources of additional information publications, trade associations, professional organizations, government agencies		

Sheet 7 – Making career contacts

Purpose: To create a guide of professional contacts.

Instructions: Record the requested information for use in researching career areas and employment opportunities.

For use with
Personal Finance
Sixth Ed., Kapoor,
Dlabay & Hughes
Page 47

Name _____

Organization _____

Address _____

_____

Phone _____ Fax _____

Web site _____ e-mail _____

Date of contact _____

Situation _____

Career situation of contact _____

Areas of specialization _____

Major accomplishments _____

Name _____

Organization _____

Address _____

_____

Phone _____ Fax _____

Web site _____ e-mail _____

Date of contact _____

Situation _____

Career situation of contact _____

Areas of specialization _____

Major accomplishments _____

Sheet 8 – Résumé worksheet

Purpose: To inventory your education, training, work background, and other experiences for use when preparing a résumé.

Instructions: List dates, organizations, and other data for each of the categories given below.

For use with
Personal Finance
Sixth Ed., Kapoor,
Dlabay & Hughes
Page 49

Education

Degree/programs completed	School/location	Dates

Work experience

Title	Organization	Dates	Responsibilities

Other experience

Title	Organization	Dates	Responsibilities

Campus/community activities

Organization/locations	Dates	Involvement

Honors/awards

Title	Organization/location	Dates

References

Name	Title	Organization	Address	Phone

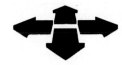

Sheet 9 – Planning a cover letter

Purpose: To outline an employment cover letter.

Instructions: Prepare the preliminary draft of a cover letter for a specific employment position.

For use with
Personal Finance
Sixth Ed., Kapoor,
Dlabay & Hughes
Page 49

Name _____

Title _____

Organization _____

Address _____

_____

Phone _____

Fax _____   e-mail _____

Information about
employment position
available _____

Organizational
information _____

Introduction: get attention of reader with distinctive skills or experience; or make reference to a mutual contact

Development: emphasize how your experience, knowledge and skills will benefit the needs of the organization in the future

Conclusion: request an interview; restate any distinctive qualities; tell how you may be contacted

Sheet 10 – Researching a prospective employer

Purpose: To obtain information about an organization for which an employment position is available.

Instructions: Use library research, informational interview, and other sources to obtain the information requested below.

For use with
Personal Finance
Sixth Ed., Kapoor,
Dlabay & Hughes
Pages 49–51

Organization _____

Address _____
_____

Contact _____

Title _____

Phone _____

Fax _____ e-mail _____

Web site _____

Title of position _____

Major products, services and customers

Locations of main offices, factories and other facilities

Major historical developments of the company

Recent company and industry developments

Required skills and experience

Major responsibilities and duties

Employee benefits

Other comments

Sheet 11 – Preparing for an interview

Purpose: To organize information and ideas for a job interview.

Instructions: Prepare information for the items listed.

For use with
Personal Finance
Sixth Ed., Kapoor,
Dlabay & Hughes
Pages 49–51

Organization _____

Address _____
_____

Contact _____

Title _____

Phone _____

Fax _____ e-mail _____

Title of position _____

Date/time/location
of interview _____

Required skills and experiences

Major responsibilities and duties

Questions you expect to be asked

Major ideas you plan to emphasize

Questions you plan to ask

Other comments

Sheet 12 – Employee benefits comparison

Purpose: To access the financial and personal value of employment benefits.

Instructions: When comparing different employment situations, or when selecting benefits, consider the factors listed below.

For use with
Personal Finance
Sixth Ed., Kapoor,
Dlabay & Hughes
Page 52

Organization		
Location		
Phone		
Contact/Title		
Health insurance Company/coverage Cost to be paid by employee		
Disability income insurance Company/coverage Cost to be paid by employee		
Life insurance Company/coverage Cost to be paid by employee		
Pension/retirement Employer contributions Vesting period Tax benefits Employee contributions		
Other benefits/estimated market value • vacation time • tuition reimbursement • child/dependent care • other		

Sheet 13 – Career development & advancement

Purpose: To develop a plan for career advancement.

Instructions: Prepare responses for the items listed.

For use with
Personal Finance
Sixth Ed., Kapoor,
Dlabay & Hughes
Pages 54–56

Current position _____

Address _____

_____

Phone _____

Fax _____   e-mail _____

Current responsibilities and duties

_____

Accomplishments

_____

Career goal within the next year

_____

Required skills and experience

_____

Plans to achieve that goal

_____

Career goal within the next two years

_____

Required skills and experience

_____

Plans to achieve that goal

_____

Career goal within the next five years

_____

Required skills and experience

_____

Plans to achieve that goal

Section C

Money management and budgeting

The worksheets in this section are to be used with Chapter 3 of *Personal Finance*, Sixth Edition.

Web sites for Financial Recordkeeping, Budgeting

Standard & Poors personal finance site	www.personalwealth.com
FinanCenter	www.financenter.com
Consumer Expenditure Survey	www.stats.bls.gov
Goal-setting tips	www.quicken.com
Budgeting information	www.lifeadvice.com
	www.americanexpress.com/student
National Center for Financial Education	www.ncfe.com
Savings information	www.savingsnet.com

Sheet 14 – Financial documents & records

Purpose: To develop a system for maintaining and storing personal financial documents and records.

Instructions: Indicate the location of the following records, and create files for the eight major categories of financial documents.

For use with
Personal Finance
Sixth Ed., Kapoor,
Dlabay & Hughes
Pages 72, 73

Item	Home file	Safe deposit box	Other (specify)
Money management records budget, financial statements			
Personal/employment records current résumé, social security card			
educational transcripts			
birth, marriage, divorce certificates			
citizenship, military papers			
adoption, custody papers			
Tax records			
Financial services/consumer credit records unused, cancelled checks			
savings, passbook statements			
savings certificates			
credit card information, statements			
credit contracts			
Consumer purchase, housing, and automobile records			
warranties, receipts			
owner's manuals			
lease or mortgage papers, title deed, property tax info			
automobile title			
auto registration			
auto service records			
Insurance records			
insurance policies			
home inventory			
medical information (health history)			
Investment records			
broker statements			
dividend reports			
stock/bond certificates			
rare coins, stamps and collectibles			
Estate planning and retirement will			
pension, social security info			

Sheet 15 – Personal balance sheet
Purpose: To determine your current financial position.
Instructions: List the current values of the asset categories below; list the amounts owed for various liabilities; subtract total liabilities from total assets to determine net worth.

For use with
Personal Finance
Sixth Ed., Kapoor,
Dlabay & Hughes
Pages 74–77

balance sheet as of _____

Assets
Liquid assets
Checking account balance _____
Savings/money market accounts, funds _____
Cash value of life insurance _____
Other _____ _____
Total liquid assets _____

Household assets & possessions
Current market value of home _____
Market value of automobiles _____
Furniture _____
Stereo, video, camera equipment _____
Jewelry _____
Other _____ _____
Other _____ _____
Total household assets _____

Investment assets
Savings certificates _____
Stocks and bonds _____
Individual retirement accounts _____
Mutual funds _____
Other _____ _____
Total investment assets _____

Total Assets ································ _____

Liabilities
Current liabilities
Charge account and credit card balances _____
Loan balances _____
Other _____ _____
Other _____ _____
Total current liabilities _____

Long-term liabilities
Mortgage _____
Other _____ _____
Total long-term liabilities _____

Total Liabilities ································ _____

Net Worth
(assets minus liabilities) _____

Sheet 16 – Personal cash flow statement
Purpose: To maintain a record of cash inflows and outflows for a month (or three months).
Instructions: Record inflows and outflows of cash f for a one (or three) month period.

For use with
Personal Finance
Sixth Ed., Kapoor,
Dlabay & Hughes
Pages 77–80

for month ending _____

Cash Inflows

Salary (take-home) _____

Other income: _____

Other income: _____

Total Income _____

Cash Outflows

Fixed expenses

Mortgage or rent _____

Loan payments _____

Insurance _____

Other _____ _____

Other _____ _____

Total fixed outflows _____

Variable expenses _____

Food _____

Clothing _____

Electricity _____

Telephone _____

Water _____

Transportation _____

Personal care _____

Medical expenses _____

Recreation/entertainment _____

Gifts _____

Donations _____

Other _____ _____

Other _____ _____

Total variable outflows _____

Total Outflows _____

Surplus/Deficit _____

Allocation of surplus

Emergency fund savings _____

Financial goals savings _____

Other savings _____ _____

Sheet 17 – Cash budget

Purpose: To compare projected an actual spending for a one (or three) month period.

Instructions: Estimate projected spending based on your cash flow statement, and maintain records for actual spending for these same budget categories.

For use with *Personal Finance* Sixth Ed., Kapoor, Dlabay & Hughes Pages 81–87

Income	Budgeted amounts dollar	Budgeted amounts percent	Actual amounts	Variance
Salary				
Other _____				
Total income		100%		
Expenses				
Fixed expenses Mortgage or rent				
Property taxes				
Loan payments				
Insurance				
Other _____				
Total fixed expenses				
Emergency fund/savings Emergency fund				
Savings for _____				
Savings for _____				
Total savings				
Variable expenses Food				
Utilities				
Clothing				
Transportation costs				
Personal care				
Medical and health care				
Entertainment				
Education				
Gifts/donations				
Miscellaneous				
Other _____				
Other _____				
Total variable expenses				
Total expenses		100%		

Sheet 18 – Annual budget summary

Purpose: To see an overview of spending patterns for a year.
Instructions: Record the monthly budget amount in the first column and actual monthly spending in the appropriate column.

For use with *Personal Finance* Sixth Ed., Kapoor, Dlabay & Hughes Page 88

Expense	Monthly Budget Amount	Jan	Feb	Mar	Apr	May	Jun
Savings							
Mortgage/rent							
Housing costs							
Telephone							
Food (at home)							
Food (away)							
Clothing							
Transportation							
Credit payments							
Insurance							
Health care							
Recreation							
Reading/education							
Gifts/donations							
Miscellaneous							
Other _____							
Other _____							
Total							

Sheet 18 (continued)

Expense	Jul	Aug	Sep	Oct	Nov	Dec	Year Totals Actual	Year Totals Budget
Savings								
Mortgage/rent								
Housing costs								
Telephone								
Food (at home)								
Food (away)								
Clothing								
Transportation								
Credit payments								
Insurance								
Health care								
Recreation								
Reading/education								
Gifts/donations								
Miscellaneous								
Other _____								
Other _____								
TOTAL								

Sheet 19 – College education cost analysis, savings plan

Purpose: To estimate future costs of college and calculate needed savings.

Instructions: Complete the information and calculations requested below.

Estimated cost of college education

Current cost of college education $ _____
(including tuition, fees, room, board, books, travel and other expenses)

Future value for _____ years until starting college at an unexpected annual inflation of _____ percent (use future value of $1, Exhibit C-1 in Appendix C) $ _____

Projected future cost of college adjusted for inflation   **(A)** $ _____

Estimated annual savings to

Projected future cost of college for inflation   **(A)** $ _____

Future value of a series of deposits for _____ years until starting college and expected annual rate of return on saving and investments of _____ percent (use Exhibit C-2 in Appendix C)   **(B)** $ _____

Estimated annual deposit to achieve needed education fund

A divided by **B** $ _____

Section D

Tax planning

The worksheets in this section are to be used with Chapter 4 of *Personal Finance*, Sixth Edition.

Sheet 20   Current income tax estimate

Sheet 21   Income tax preparer comparison

Sheet 22   Tax planning activities

Web sites for Tax Planning

Internal Revenue Service	www.irs.gov
Tax forms & tips	www.1040.com
	www.taxweb.com
File your taxes online	www.taxsoft.com
Ernst & Young	www.ey.com/us/tax
H&R Block	www.hrblock.com
Turbo Tax	www.intuit.com/turbotax
State income tax information	www.taxadmin.org

Sheet 20 – Current income tax estimate

Purpose: To estimate your current federal income tax liability.

Instructions: Based on last year's tax return, estimates for the current year, and current tax regulations and rates, estimate your current tax liability.

For use with
Personal Finance
Sixth Ed., Kapoor,
Dlabay & Hughes
Pages 99–104

Gross income (wages, salary, investment income, and other ordinary income		$	
Less Adjustments to income (see current tax regulations)		- $	
Equals Adjusted gross income		= $	
Less Standard deduction **or**	Itemized deduction		
	medical expenses (exceeding 7.5% of AGI)		$
	state/local income, property taxes		$
	mortgage, home equity loan		$
	interest		$
	contributions		$
	casualty and theft losses		$
	moving expenses, job-related and miscellaneous expenses (exceeding 2% of AGI)		$
Amount - $	**Total**		- $
Less Personal exemptions		- $	
Equals Taxable income		= $	
Estimated tax (based on current tax tables or tax schedules)		$	
Less Tax credits		- $	
Plus Other taxes		+ $	
Equals Total tax liability		= $	
Less Estimated withholding and payments		- $	
Equals Tax due (or refund)		= $	

Sheet 21 – Income tax preparer comparison

Purpose: To compare the services and costs of different income tax return preparation sources.

Instructions: Using advertisements and information from tax preparation services, obtain information for the following.

For use with *Personal Finance* Sixth Ed., Kapoor, Dlabay & Hughes Pages 116, 117

	Local tax service	National tax service	Local accountant
Company name			
Address			
Telephone			
Web site			
Cost of preparation of Form 1040EZ			
Cost of preparation of Form 1040A			
Cost of preparation of Form 1040 with Schedule A (itemized deductions)			
Cost of preparation of state or local tax return			
Cost of electronic filing			
Assistance provided if IRS questions your return			
Other services provided			

Sheet 22 – Tax planning activities

Purpose: To consider actions that can prevent tax penalties and may result in tax savings.

Instructions: Consider which of the following actions are appropriate to your tax situation.

For use with Personal Finance Sixth Ed., Kapoor, Dlabay & Hughes Pages 119,120

	Action to be taken (if applicable)	Completed
Filing status/withholding		
Change filing status or exemptions due to changes in life situation		
Change amount of withholding due to changes in tax situations		
Plan to make estimated tax payments (due the 15th of April, June, September, and January)		
Tax records/documents		
Organize home files for ease of maintaining and retrieving data		
Send current mailing address, correct social security number to IRS, place of employment, and other income sources		
Annual tax activities		
Be certain all needed data and current tax forms are available well before deadline		
Research tax code changes and uncertain tax areas		
Tax savings actions		
Consider tax-exempt and tax-deferred investments		
If you expect to have the same or lower tax rate next year, accelerate deductions into the current year		
If you expect to have the same or lower tax rate next year, delay the receipt of income until next year		
If you expect to have a higher tax rate next year, delay deductions since they will have a greater benefit		
If you expect to have a higher tax rate next year, accelerate the receipt of income to have it taxed at the current lower rate		
Start or increase use of tax-deferred retirements plans		
Other		

Section E

Banking services

The worksheets in this section are to be used with Chapter 5 of *Personal Finance*, Sixth Edition.

Web sites for Banking Services

Current rates for savings instruments	www.bankrate.com/bankrate/publ/tips.htm
	www.banx.com
	www.usatoday.com/money/savebox.htm
Federal Deposit Insurance Corporation	www.fdic.gov
U.S. Saving Bonds	www.publicdebt.treas.gov/sav/sav.htm
Federal Reserve System	www.bog.frb.fed.us
Purchasing government notes & bonds	www.frbsf.org
Current value of U.S. savings bonds	www.ny.frb.org
American Bankers Assn.	www.aba.com
Financial calculators for savings	www.centura.com/formulas/ca/c.html
Making payments on the Internet	www.checkfree.com
Online banking information	www.orcc.com/banking.htm/

Sheet 23 – Planning the use of financial services

Purpose: To indicate currently used financial services and to determine services that may be needed in the future.

Instructions: List (1) currently used services with financial institution information (name, address, phone); and (2) services that are likely to be needed in the future.

For use with
Personal Finance
Sixth Ed., Kapoor,
Dlabay & Hughes
Pages 132, 133

Types of financial services	Current financial services used	Additional financial services needed
Payment services (checking, cash machine, money orders)	Financial Institution	
Savings services (savings account, certificate of deposit, savings bonds)	Financial Institution	
Credit services (credit cards, personal loans, mortgage)	Financial Institution	
Other financial services (investments, trust account, tax planning)	Financial Institution	

Sheet 24 – Using savings to achieve financial goals

Purpose: To monitor savings for use in reaching financial goals.
Instructions: Record savings plan information along with the amount of your balance or income on a periodic basis.

For use with
Personal Finance
Sixth Ed., Kapoor,
Dlabay & Hughes
Pages 142–146

Regular savings account
Acct. No _____

Savings goal/Amount needed/Date needed:

Financial institution

_____

Address _____

_____

Phone _____

Initial deposit:	Date _____	$ _____
Balance:	Date _____	$ _____
	Date _____	$ _____
	Date _____	$ _____
	Date _____	$ _____

Certificate of deposit
Acct. No _____

Savings goal/Amount needed/Date needed:

Financial institution

_____

Address _____

_____

Phone _____

Initial deposit:	Date _____	$ _____
Balance:	Date _____	$ _____
	Date _____	$ _____
	Date _____	$ _____
	Date _____	$ _____

Money market/fund acct.
Acct. No _____

Savings goal/Amount needed/Date needed:

Financial institution

_____

Address _____

_____

Phone _____

Initial deposit:	Date _____	$ _____
Balance:	Date _____	$ _____
	Date _____	$ _____
	Date _____	$ _____
	Date _____	$ _____

U.S. Savings Bonds
Purchase location _____

Savings goal/Amount needed/Date needed:

Address _____

_____

Phone _____

Purchase date: _____	Maturity date: _____
Amount: _____	Maturity date: _____
Purchase date: _____	Maturity date: _____
Amount: _____	Maturity date: _____

Other Savings
Acct. No _____

Savings goal/Amount needed/Date needed:

Financial institution

_____

Address _____

_____

Phone _____

Initial deposit:	Date _____	$ _____
Balance:	Date _____	$ _____
	Date _____	$ _____
	Date _____	$ _____
	Date _____	$ _____

Sheet 25 – Savings plan comparison

Purpose: To compare the benefits and costs associated with different savings plans.

Instructions: Analyze advertisements and contact various financial institutions to obtain the information requested below.

For use with *Personal Finance* Sixth Ed., Kapoor, Dlabay & Hughes Pages 146–149

Type of savings plan (regular passbook account, special accounts, savings certificate, money market account, other)			
Financial institution			
Address/Phone			
Web site			
Annual interest rate			
Annual percentage yield (APY)			
Frequency of compounding			
Interest computation method • day of deposit, day of withdrawal • average daily balance • low balance • other_____			
Insured by FDIC, NCUA, other			
Maximum amount insured			
Minimum initial deposit			
Minimum time period savings must be on deposit			
Penalties for early withdrawal			
Service charges/fees transaction fee for more than set number of withdrawals			
Other costs/fees			
"Free" gifts (item, amount of deposit, interest lost)			

Sheet 26 – Checking account comparison

Purpose: To compare the benefits and costs associated with different checking accounts.

Instructions: Analyze advertisements and contact various financial institutions (banks, savings and loan associations, or credit unions) to obtain the information requested below.

For use with *Personal Finance* Sixth Ed., Kapoor, Dlabay & Hughes Pages 150–152

Institution name			
Address			
Phone			
Web site			
Type of account (regular checking, interest-earning account, or other)			
Minimum balance for "free" checking			
Monthly charge for going below minimum balance			
"Free" checking accounts for full-time students?			
On-line banking services			
Other fees/costs printing of checks			
stop payment order			
overdrawn account			
certified check			
ATM, other charges			
Banking hours			
Location of branch offices and ATM terminals			

Sheet 27 – Checking account cost analysis

Purpose: To compare the inflows and outflows of a checking account.

Instructions: Record the interest earned (inflows) and the costs and fees (outflows) as requested below. *Note: Not all items will apply to every checking account.*

For use with *Personal Finance* Sixth Ed., Kapoor, Dlabay & Hughes Page 154

Inflows

Step 1

Multiply average monthly balance $ _____ by average rate of return _____ % to determine annual earnings

Outflows

Step 2

Monthly service charge
$ _____ X 12 = $ _____

Average number of checks written per month _____ X charge per check (if applicable) X 12 = $ _____

Average number of deposits per month _____ X charge per deposit (if applicable) X 12 = $ _____

Fee incurred when going below minimum balance _____ X times below minimum = $ _____

Lost interest: opportunity cost _____ % X required minimum balance $ _____ = $ _____

= [_____]

Total Estimated Inflow
$ _____

Total Estimated Outflow
$ _____

> **Estimated inflows less outflows =**
> **Net earnings for account_____**
> **-Net cost for account _____**
> **+/- $** _____

Note: *This calculation does not take into account charges and fees for such services as overdrafts, stop payments, ATM use, and check printing. Be sure to also consider those costs when selecting a checking account.*

Sheet 28 – Checking account reconciliation

Purpose: To determine the adjusted cash balance for your checking account.

Instructions: Enter data from your bank statement and checkbook for the amounts requested.

For use with
Personal Finance
Sixth Ed., Kapoor,
Dlabay & Hughes
Page 162

Date of bank statement _____ ,

Balance on bank statement $ _____

Step 1
Subtract total of outstanding checks (checks that you have written but have not yet cleared in the banking system)

Check No.	Amount	Check No.	Amount
_____	_____	_____	_____
_____	_____	_____	_____
_____	_____	_____	_____
_____	_____	_____	_____

                                                                -$ _____

Step 2
Add deposits in transit (deposits you have made but have not been reported on this statement)

Date	Amount	Date	Amount
_____	_____	_____	_____
_____	_____	_____	_____

                                      +$ _____

Adjusted cash balance $ _____

Current balance in your checkbook   _____

Step 3
Subtract fees or other charges listed on your bank statement

Item	Amount	Item	Amount
_____	_____	_____	_____
_____	_____	_____	_____

                                                                -$ _____

Step 4
Add interest earned   +$ _____
Add direct deposits   +$ _____

                                      Adjusted cash balance $ _____

(The two adjusted balances should be the same; if not, carefully check your math and check to see that deposits and checks recorded in your checkbook and on your statement are for the correct amounts.)

Section F

Consumer credit

The worksheet in this section are to be used with Chapters 6 and 7 of *Personal Finance*, Sixth Edition.

Sheet 29   Consumer credit usage patterns (debt inventory)

Sheet 30   Credit card/charge account comparison

Sheet 31   Consumer loan comparison

Web sites for Using Credit Wisely and comparing Credit Costs

RAM Research Group	www.ramresearch.com
Comparison of costs & features	www.cardtrak.com
Current loan & credit card rates	www.bankrate.com
	www.bankx.com
Nat'l Center for Financial Education	www.ncfe.org
Credit reports information	www.equifax.com
	www.experian.com
	www.tuc.com
Consumer Credit law information	www.ftc.gov
	www.federalreserve.gov
	www.pirg.org
FinanCenter	www.financenter.com
Nat'l Found. for Consumer Credit	www.nfcc.org
Nat'l Credit Counseling Services	www.nccs.org
Debt Counselors of America	www.dca.org
Credit cost calculators	www.centura.com/formulas/calc.html

Sheet 29 – Consumer credit usage patterns

Purpose: To create a record of current consumer debt balances.
Instructions: Record account names, numbers, and payments for current consumer debts.

For use with
Personal Finance
Sixth Ed., Kapoor,
Dlabay & Hughes
Pages 166, 167

Date _____

Automobile, education, personal and installment loans

Financial institution	Account number	Current balance	Monthly payment
_____	_____	_____	_____
_____	_____	_____	_____
_____	_____	_____	_____
_____	_____	_____	_____
_____	_____	_____	_____

Charge accounts and credit cards

_____	_____	_____	_____
_____	_____	_____	_____
_____	_____	_____	_____
_____	_____	_____	_____
_____	_____	_____	_____
_____	_____	_____	_____
_____	_____	_____	_____
_____	_____	_____	_____

Other loans (overdraft protection, home equity, life insurance loan)

_____	_____	_____	_____
_____	_____	_____	_____
_____	_____	_____	_____
_____	_____	_____	_____

Totals _____ _____

Debt payment-to-income ratio $= \dfrac{\text{Total montly payments}}{\text{net (after} - \text{tax) income}}$

Sheet 30 - Credit card/charge account comparison

Purpose: To compare the benefits and costs associated with different credit cards and charge accounts.

Instructions: Analyze ads, credit applications, and contact various financial institutions to obtain the information requested below.

For use with
Personal Finance
Sixth Ed., Kapoor,
Dlabay & Hughes
Pages 169–174

Type of credit/charge account			
Name of company/account			
Address/phone			
Web site			
Type of purchases which can be made			
Annual fee (if any)			
Annual percentage rate (APR) (interest calculation information)			
Credit limit for new customers			
Minimum monthly payment			
Other costs: credit report late fee other_____			
Restrictions (age, minimum annual income)			
Other information for consumers to consider			
Frequent flyer or other bonus points			

Sheet 31 – Consumer loan comparison

Purpose: To compare the costs associated with different sources of consumer loans.

Instructions: Contact or visit a bank, credit union, and consumer finance company to obtain information on a loan for a specific purpose.

For use with
Personal Finance
Sixth Ed., Kapoor,
Dlabay & Hughes
Pages 176–178

Type of financial institution			
Name			
Address			
Phone			
Web site			
Amount of down payment			
Length of loan (months)			
What collateral is required?			
Amount of monthly payment			
Total amount to be repaid (monthly amount x number of months + down payment)			
Total finance charge/cost of credit			
Annual percentage rate (APR)			
Other costs credit life insurance credit report other costs			
Is a co-signer required?			
Other information			

Section G

Consumer buying

The worksheets in this section are to be used with Chapter 8 of *Personal Finance*, Sixth Edition.

Web sites for Consumer Buying, Transportation

Consumer Reports	www.consumerreports.org
Consumer topics	www.consumerworld.org
Brand, price, and feature comparisons	www.compare.net
	www.pricescan.com
Government information sources	www.consumer.gov
	www.pueblo.gsa.gov
	www.ftc.gov
National Fraud Information Center	www.fraud.org
Better Business Bureau	www.bbb.org
Legal information for consumers	www.nolo.com
	www.consumerlaw.org
	www.consumerlawpage.com
Prices of new and used cars	www.edmunds.com
	www.kbb.com
Leasing information	www.leasesource.com
Driving safety information	www.hwysafety.com
Crash test and insurance-related data	www.carsafety.org

Sheet 32 - Comparing cash and credit for major purchases

Purpose: To compare the costs and benefits of cash and credit.

Instructions: When considering a major consumer purchase, complete the information requested below.

For use with
Personal Finance
Sixth Ed., Kapoor,
Dlabay & Hughes
Pages 244–246

Item/Description _____

Cash price

Selling price	$	_____
Sales tax	$	_____
Additional charges (delivery, setup, service contract)	$	_____
Discounts (employee, senior citizen or student discounts, discounts for paying cash)	$	-_____
Net cost of item times percent interest that could be earned times years of use to determine opportunity cost	$	_____

Total financial & economic cost when paying cash $ [_____]

Credit price

Down payment	$	_____
Financing: monthly payment times months	$	_____
Additional financing charges (application fee, credit report, credit life insurance)	$	_____
Product-related charges (delivery, setup)	$	_____
Discounts that may apply	$	-_____

Total financial & economic cost when using credit $ [_____]

Other considerations

Will cash used for the purchase be needed for other purposes?

Will this credit purchase result in financial difficulties?

Do alternatives exist for this purchasing and payment decision?

Note: Use Sheet 33 to compare brands, stores, features and prices when making a major consumer purchase.

Sheet 33 – Consumer purchase comparison

Purpose: To research and evaluate brands and store services for purchase of a major consumer item.

Instructions: When considering the purchase of a major consumer item, use ads, catalogs, the World Wide Web, store visits and other sources to obtain the information below.

For use with *Personal Finance* Sixth Ed., Kapoor, Dlabay & Hughes Page 246

Product

Exact description (size, model, features, etc.)

Research the item in consumer periodicals with information regarding your product

article/periodical _____   **article/periodical** _____

date/pages _____   **date/pages** _____

What buying suggestions are presented in the articles?

Which brands are recommended in these articles? Why?

Contact or visit two or three stores that sell the product to obtain the following information:

	Store 1	Store 2	Store 3
Store name			
Address			
Phone			
Brand name/cost			
Product difference from item above			
Guarantee/warranty offered (describe)			

Which brand and at which store would you buy this product? Why?

Sheet 34 – Unit pricing worksheet

Purpose: to calculate the unit price for a consumer purchase.
Instructions: Use advertisements or information obtained during store visits to calculate and compare unit prices.

For use with
Personal Finance
Sixth Ed., Kapoor,
Dlabay & Hughes
Page 249

Item _____

Date	Store/Location	Brand	Total price	÷	Size	=	Unit Price	Unit of Measurement
____	_____	_____	_____		____		_____	_____
____	_____	_____	_____		____		_____	_____
____	_____	_____	_____		____		_____	_____
____	_____	_____	_____		____		_____	_____
____	_____	_____	_____		____		_____	_____

Highest unit price
Store _____
Date _____

Lowest unit price
Store _____
Date _____
Difference: _____

Wisest consumer buy/best overall store

_____

Reasons

Sheet 35 - Legal services cost comparison

Purpose: To compare costs of services from different sources of legal assistance.

Instructions: Contact various sources of legal services (lawyer, prepaid legal service, legal aid society) to compare costs and available services.

For use with *Personal Finance* Sixth Ed., Kapoor, Dlabay & Hughes Page 256

Type of legal service			
Organization Name			
Address			
Phone			
Web site			
Contact person			
Recommended by			
Areas of specialization			
Cost of initial consultation			
Cost of simple will			
Cost of real estate closing			
Cost method for other services—flat fee, hourly rate, or contingency basis			
Other information			

Sheet 36 – Current and future transportation needs

Purpose: To assess current and future transportation.

Instructions: Based on current needs and expected needs, complete the information requested below.

For use with
Personal Finance
Sixth Ed., Kapoor,
Dlabay & Hughes
Page 262

Current situation: Date _____

Vehicle 1

Year/Model	_____
Mileage	_____
Condition	_____
Needed repairs	_____

Estimated annual costs

gas, oil, repairs	_____
insurance	_____
loan balance	_____
Est. market value	_____

Vehicle 2

Year/Model	_____
Mileage	_____
Condition	_____
Needed repairs	_____

Estimated annual costs

gas, oil, repairs	_____
insurance	_____
loan balance	_____
Est. market value	_____

Expected and projected changes in transportation needs

Personal desires and concerns regarding current transportation

Analysis of future desired transportation situation
Description of new vehicle situation

Time when this situation is desired

Financing resources needed

Available and projected financial resources

Concerns that must be overcome

Realistic time when transportation of choice may be achieved

Sheet 37 - Used car purchase comparison

Purpose: To research and evaluate different types and sources of used cars.

Instructions: When considering a used car purchase, use advertisements and visits to new and used car dealers to obtain the information below.

For use with *Personal Finance* Sixth Ed., Kapoor, Dlabay & Hughes Page 264

Automobile (year, make, model)			
Name			
Address			
Phone			
Web site			
Cost			
Mileage			
Condition of auto			
Condition of tires			
Radio			
Air conditioning			
Other options			
Warranty (describe)			
Items in need of repair			
Inspection items:			
• any rust, major dents?			
• oil or fluid leaks?			
• condition of brakes?			
• proper operation of heater, wipers, other accessories?			
Other information			

Sheet 38 – Buying vs. leasing and automobile

Purpose: To compare costs of buying and leasing an automobile or other vehicle.

Instructions: Obtain costs related to leasing and buying a vehicle.

For use with
Personal Finance
Sixth Ed., Kapoor,
Dlabay & Hughes
Page 269

Purchase costs

Total vehicle cost, including sales tax ($ _____)

Down payment (or full amount if paying cash) $ _____

Monthly loan payment $ _____ times _____ month loan
(this item is zero if vehicle is not finances) $ _____

Opportunity cost of down payment (or total cost of the vehicle if bought for cash)

$ _____ times number of years of financing/ownership times
_____ percent (interest rate which funds could earn) $ _____

Less: estimated value of vehicle at end of loan term/ownership $ _____

Total Cost to Buy .... $ _____

Leasing costs

Security deposit $ _____

Monthly lease payments $ _____ times _____ months $ _____

Opportunity cost of security deposit:

$ _____ times _____ years times _____ percent $ _____

End-of-lease charges (if applicable*) $ _____

Total Cost to Lease .... $ _____

*With a closed-end lease, charges for extra mileage or excessive wear and tear; with an open-end lease, end-of-lease payment if appraised value is less than estimated ending value.

Sheet 39 – Auto ownership and operation costs

Purpose: To calculate or estimate the cost of owning and operating an automobile or other vehicle.

Instructions: Maintain records related to the cost of categories listed below

For use with
Personal Finance
Sixth Ed., Kapoor,
Dlabay & Hughes
Pages 271–273

Model year _____   Make, size, model _____

Fixed ownership costs

Depreciation*
Purchase price $ _____ divided by estimated life of _____ years $ _____

Interest on auto loan
Annual cost of financing vehicle if buying on credit $ _____

Insurance for the vehicle
Annual cost of liability and property $ _____

License, registration fee and taxes $ _____
Cost of registering vehicle for state and city license fees $ _____

Total Fixed Costs .... $ _____

Variable costs

Gasoline
_____ estimated miles per year divided by _____ miles per gallon
of _____ times the average price of $ _____ per gallon $ _____

Oil changes
Cost of regular oil changes during the year $ _____

Tires
Cost of tires purchased during the year $ _____

Maintenance/repairs
Cost of planned or other expected maintenance $ _____

Parking and tolls
Regular fees for parking and highway toll charges $ _____

Total Variable Costs .... $ _____

Total costs $ _____

Divided by miles per year _____

Equals cost per mile $ _____

(*This estimate of vehicle depreciation is based on a straight-line approach–equal depreciation year; a more realistic approach would be larger amounts in the early years ownership, such as 25-30% in the first year, 30-35% in the second; most cars lose 90 percent of their value by the time they are seven years old.)

Section H

Housing

The worksheets in this section are to be used with Chapter 9 of *Personal Finance*, Sixth Edition.

Web sites for Housing

Renting vs. buying	www.financenter.com
Home buying guide	www.maxsol.com/homes/steps/htm
Home buying assistance	www.homefair.com/home
	www.town.com
	www.realestate.com
	www.ired.com
Mortgage information	www.bankrate.com
	www.homeshark.com
	www.hsh.com
	www.lendingtree.com
	www.eloan.com
Adjustable rate mortgages	www.maxol.com/homes/comparm/htm
FNMA (Fannie Mae)	www.homepath.com
Dept. of Housing & Urban Development	www.hud.gov
Mortgage pre-payment information	www.alfredo.wustl.edu/mort/
Reverse mortgages	www.hud.gov/rvrsmort.html
Mortgage cost calculator	www.centura.com/formulas/calc.html

For use with
Personal Finance
Sixth Ed., Kapoor,
Dlabay & Hughes
Page 279

Sheet 40 – Current and future housing needs

Purpose: To assess current and future plans for housing.
Instructions: Based on current and expected future needs, complete the information requested below.

Current situation: **Date** _____

Renting   ## Buying

Location _____   Location _____

Description _____   Description _____

_____   _____

Advantages _____   Advantages _____

_____   _____

Disadvantages _____   Disadvantages _____

_____   _____

Rent $ _____   Mortgage payment $ _____

Lease expiration _____   Balance $ _____

                                             Current market value _____

Expected and projected changes in housing needs
_____

Personal desires and concerns regarding current housing situation
_____

Analysis of future desired housing situation

Description of new housing situation	
Time when this situation is desired	
Financing resources needed/available	
Concerns that must be overcome	
Realistic time when transportation of choice may be achieved	

Sheet 41 - Renting vs. buying housing

Purpose: To compare cost of renting and buying your place of residence.

Instructions: Obtain estimates for comparable housing units for the data requested below.

For use with
Personal Finance
Sixth Ed., Kapoor,
Dlabay & Hughes
Page 280

Rental costs

Annual rent payments (monthly rent $ _____ X 12)	$	_____
Renter's insurance	$	_____
Interest lost on security deposit	$	_____
(deposit times after-tax savings acct. interest rate)		

Total Annual Cost of Renting $ _____

Buying costs

Annual mortgage payments	$	_____
Property taxes (annual costs)	$	_____
Homeowner's insurance (annual premium)	$	_____
Estimated maintenance and repairs	$	_____
After-tax interest lost because of down payment and closing costs	$	_____

Less: *financial benefits of home ownership*

Growth in equity	$-	_____
Tax savings for mortgage interest	$-	_____
(annual mortgage interest times tax rate)		
Tax savings for property taxes	$-	_____
(annual property taxes times tax rate)		
Estimated annual depreciation	$-	_____

Total Annual Cost of Buying $ _____

Sheet 42 - Apartment rental comparison

Purpose: To evaluate and compare rental housing alternatives.
Instructions: When in the market for an apartment, obtain information to compare costs and facilities of three apartments.

For use with
Personal Finance
Sixth Ed., Kapoor,
Dlabay & Hughes
Page 286

Name of renting person or apartment building			
Address			
Phone			
Monthly rent			
Amount of security deposit			
Length of lease			
Utilities included in rent			
Parking facilities			
Storage area in building			
Laundry facilities			
Distance to schools			
Distance to public transportation			
Distance to shopping			
Pool, recreation area, other facilities			
Estimated other costs:			
Electric			
Telephone			
Gas			
Water			
Other costs			
Other information			

Sheet 43 – Housing affordability and mortgage qualification

For use with
Personal Finance
Sixth Ed., Kapoor,
Dlabay & Hughes
Pages 294

Purpose: To estimate the amount of affordable mortgage payment, mortgage amount, and home purchase price.

Instructions: Enter the amounts requested, and perform the required calculations.

Step 1
Determine your monthly gross income (annual income divided by 12)

$ _____

Step 2
With a down payment of at least 10 percent, lenders use 28 percent of monthly gross income as a guideline for TIPI (taxes, insurance, principal and interest), 36 percent of monthly gross income as a guideline for TIPI plus other debt payments (enter .28 or .36)

X _____

Step 3
Subtract other debt payments (such as payments on an auto loan), if applicable

- _____

Subtract estimated monthly costs of property taxes and homeowners insurance

- _____

Affordable monthly mortgage payment

$ _____

Step 4
Divide this amount by the monthly mortgage payment per $1,000 based on current mortgage rates (see Exhibit 9-9, text p.). For example, for a 10 percent , 30-year loan, the number would be $8.78)

÷ _____

Multiply by $1,000

X ___ $1,000 ___

Affordable mortgage amount

$ _____

Step 5
Divide your affordable mortgage amount by 1 minus the fractional portion of your down payment (for example, 0.9 for a 10 percent down payment)

÷ _____

Affordable home purchase price

$ _____

Note: The two ratios used by lending institutions (Step 2) and other loan requirements are likely to vary based on a variety of factors, including the type of mortgage, the amount of the down payment, your income level, and current interest rates. If you have other debts, lenders will calculate both ratios and then use the one that allows you greater flexibility in borrowing.

Sheet 44 – Mortgage company comparison

Purpose: To compare the services and costs for different home mortgage sources.

Instructions: When obtaining a mortgage, obtain the information requested below from different mortgage companies.

For use with
Personal Finance
Sixth Ed., Kapoor,
Dlabay & Hughes

Amount of mortgage	$ _____	Down payment	$ _____	Years _____

Company		
Address		
Phone		
Web site		
Contact person		
Application, credit report, property appraisal fees		
Loan origination fee		
Other fees, charges (commitment, title, tax transfer)		
Fixed rate mortgage		
Monthly payment		
Discount points		
Adjustable rate mortgage		
▪ time until first rate charge ▪ frequency of rate charge		
Monthly payment		
Discount points		
Payment cap		
Interest rate cap		
Rate index used		
Commitment period		
Other information		

Sheet 45 – Mortgage refinance analysis

Purpose: To determine savings associated with refinancing a mortgage.

Instructions: Record financing costs and amount saved with new mortgage in the areas provided.

For use with
Personal Finance
Sixth Ed., Kapoor,
Dlabay & Hughes
Page 301

Costs of refinancing:

Points	$	_____
Application fee	$	_____
Credit report	$	_____
Attorney fees	$	_____
Title search	$	_____
Title insurance	$	_____
Appraisal fee	$	_____
Inspection fee	$	_____
Other fees	$	_____

Total refinancing costs   (A) $ _____

Monthly savings:

Current monthly mortgage
payment $ _____

Less:

new monthly payment $ _____

Monthly savings   (B) $ _____

Number of months to cover finance costs

Refinance costs (A) divided by monthly savings (B)

_____ months

Section I

Insurance

The worksheets in this section are to be used with Chapters 10-12 of *Personal Finance*, Sixth Edition.

Web sites for Insurance

Insurance Research Council	www.ircweb.org
Basic insurance information	www.insure.com; www.iiaa.iix.com; www.iii.org
Rate information	www.insuremarket.com
Links to health-related sites	www.healthseek.com
Life & Health Info Foundation for Education	www.life-line.org
Health insurance options	
Medicare (Social Security Administration)	www.ssa.gov
Medicare supplement information	www.naic.org
Determining life insurance needs	www.rightquote.com
Comparing coverages and costs	www.quotesmith.com; www.quickquote.com
	wqww.accuquote.com
Life insurance information	www.insure.com
Planning assistance & rate information	www.insuremarket.com; www.lifenet.com
State insurance regulatory agencies	www.naic.org

Sheet 46 - Current insurance policies and needs

Purpose: To establish a record of current and needed insurance coverage.

Instructions: List current insurance policies and areas where new or additional coverage is needed.

For use with *Personal Finance* Sixth Ed., Kapoor, Dlabay & Hughes Page 316

Current coverage	Needed coverage
Property	
Company	
Policy No.	
Coverage amounts	
Deductible	
Annual premium	
Agent	
Address	
Phone	
Web site	
Automobile insurance	
Company	
Policy No.	
Coverage amounts	
Deductible	
Annual premium	
Agent	
Address	
Phone	
Web site	
Disability income insurance	
Company	
Policy No.	
Coverage	
Contact	
Phone	
Web site	
Health insurance	
Company	
Policy No.	
Policy provisions	
Contact	
Phone	
Web site	
Life insurance	
Company	
Policy No.	
Type of policy	
Amount of coverage	
Cash value	
Agent	
Phone	
Web site	

Sheet 47 – Home inventory
Purpose: To create a record of personal belongings for use when settling home insurance claims.
Instructions: For areas of the home, list your possessions including a description (model, serial number), cost and date of acquisition.

For use with
Personal Finance
Sixth Ed., Kapoor,
Dlabay & Hughes
Page 320

Item, description	Cost	Date acquired
Attic		
Bathroom		
Bedrooms		
Family room		
Living room		
Hallways		
Kitchen		
Dining room		
Basement		
Garage		
Other items		

Sheet 48 – Determining needed property insurance

Purpose: To determine property insurance needed for a home or apartment.

Instructions: Estimate the value and your needs for the categories below.

For use with *Personal Finance* Sixth Ed., Kapoor, Dlabay & Hughes Page 325

Real property (this section not applicable to renters)
Current replacement value of home $ _____

Personal property
Estimated value of appliances, furniture, clothing and other
household items (conduct an inventory) $ _____

Type of coverage for personal property

    actual cash value [   ]

    replacement value [   ]

Additional coverage for items with limits on standard personal property coverage such as jewelry, firearms, silverware, photographic, electronic and computer equipment

Item	Amount

Personal liability
Amount of additional personal liability coverage desired for
possible personal injury claims $ _____

Specialized coverages
If appropriate, investigate flood or earthquake coverage
excluded from home insurance policies $ _____

Note: Use Sheet 49 to compare companies, coverages and costs for apartment or home insurance.

Sheet 49 – Apartment/home insurance comparison

Purpose: To research and compare companies, coverages and costs for apartment or home insurance.

Instructions: Contact three insurance agents to obtain the information requested below.

For use with *Personal Finance* Sixth Ed., Kapoor, Dlabay & Hughes Page 326

Type of building: ☐ apartment   ☐ home   ☐ condominium

Location: _____

Type of construction _____ Age of building _____

Company name			
Agent's name, address and phone			
Coverage: Dwelling $ Other structures $ (does not apply to apartment/condo coverage)	Premium	Premium	Premium
Personal property $			
Additional living expenses $			
Personal liability Bodily injury $ Property damage $			
Medical payments per person $			
per accident $			
Deductible amount			
Other coverage $			
Service charges or fees			
Total Premium			

Sheet 50 – Automobile insurance cost comparison

Purpose: To research and compare companies, coverages and costs for auto insurance.

Instructions: Contact three insurance agents to obtain the information requested below.

For use with *Personal Finance* Sixth Ed., Kapoor, Dlabay & Hughes Page 334

Automobile (year, make, model, engine size) _____

Driver's age _____ Sex _____ Total miles driven in a year _____

Full- or part-time drive? _____Total miles driven in a year _____

Driver's education completed?_____

Accidents or violations within the past three years? _____

Company name			
Agent's name, address and phone			
Policy length (6 months, 1 year)			
Coverage:	Premium	Premium	Premium
Bodily injury liability per person $ per accident $			
Property damage liab. per accident $			
Collision deductible $			
Comprehensive deductible $			
Medical payments per person $			
Uninsured motorist per person $			
per accident $			
Other coverage			
Service charges			
Total Premium			

Sheet 51 – Disability income insurance needs

Purpose: To determine financial needs and insurance coverage related to employment disability situations.

Instructions: Use the categories below to determine your potential income needs and disability insurance coverage.

For use with *Personal Finance* Sixth Ed., Kapoor, Dlabay & Hughes Page 349

Monthly expenses

	Current	When disabled
Mortgage (or rent)	$ _____	$ _____
Utilities	$ _____	$ _____
Food	$ _____	$ _____
Clothing	$ _____	$ _____
Insurance payments	$ _____	$ _____
Debt payments	$ _____	$ _____
Auto/transportation	$ _____	$ _____
Medical/dental care	$ _____	$ _____
Education	$ _____	$ _____
Personal allowances	$ _____	$ _____
Recreation/entertainment	$ _____	$ _____
Contributions, donations	$ _____	$ _____

Total Monthly Expenses When Disabled $ _____

Substitute income

	Monthly benefit*
Group disability insurance	$ _____
Social security	$ _____
State disability insurance	$ _____
Workers' compensation	$ _____
Credit disability insurance	$ _____
(in some auto loan or home mortgages)	
Other income (investments, etc.)	$ _____

Total Projected Income When Disabled $ _____

If projected income when disabled is less than expenses, additional disability income insurance should be considered.

(*Most disability insurance programs have a waiting period before benefits start, and may have a limit as to how long benefits are received.)

Sheet 52 – Assessing current and needed health care insurance

Purpose: To assess current and needed medical and health care insurance.

Instructions: Investigate your existing medical and health insurance, and determine the need for additional coverages.

For use with
Personal Finance
Sixth Ed., Kapoor,
Dlabay & Hughes
Page 357

Insurance company

Address

Type of coverage   ☐ individual health policy   ☐ group health policy

☐ HMO   ☐ PPO   ☐ other

Premium amount (monthly/quarter/semi-annual/annual)

Main coverages

Amount of coverage for

hospital costs

surgery costs

physician's fees

lab tests

out-patient expenses

maternity

major medical

Other items covered/amounts

Policy restrictions (deductible, co-insurance, maximum limits)

Items not covered by this insurance

Of items not covered, would supplemental coverage be appropriate for your personal situation?

What actions related to your current (or proposed additional) coverage are necessary?

Sheet 53 - Determining life insurance needs

Purpose: To estimate life insurance coverage needed to cover expected expenses and future family living costs.

Instructions: Estimate the amounts requested for the categories listed.

For use with
Personal Finance
Sixth Ed., Kapoor,
Dlabay & Hughes
Page 379

Household expenses to be covered

Final expenses (funeral, estate taxes, etc.)	1	$ _____
Payment of consumer debt amounts	2	$ _____
Emergency fund	3	$ _____
College fund	4	$ _____

Expected living expenses:

Average living expense	$ _____
Spouse's income after taxes	$ - _____
Annual Social Security benefits	$ - _____
Net annual living expenses	$ _____
Years until spouse is 90	$ _____
Investment rate factor (see below)	$ _____

Total living expenses

(net annual expenses times investment rate factor)	5	$ _____

Total monetary needs (1+2+3+4+5)		$ _____
Less: Total current investments		$ _____
Life insurance needs		$ _____

Investment rate factors

Years until spouse is 90	25	30	35	40	45	50	55	60
conservative investment	20	22	25	27	30	31	33	35
aggressive investment	16	17	19	20	21	21	22	23

Note: Use Sheet 54 to compare life insurance policies.

Sheet 54 - Life insurance policy comparison

Purpose: To research and compare companies, coverages, and costs for different life insurance policies.

Instructions: Analyze ads and contact life insurance agents to obtain the information requested below.

For use with *Personal Finance* Sixth Ed., Kapoor, Dlabay & Hughes Page 398

Age:

Company			
Agent's name, address and phone			
Type of insurance (term, straight/whole, limited payment, endowment, universal)			
Type of policy (individual, group)			
Amount of coverage			
Frequency of payment (monthly, quarterly, semi-annual, annual)			
Premium amount			
Other costs: • service charges • physical exam			
Rate of return (annual percentage increase in cash value; not applicable for term policies)			
Benefits of insurance as stated in ad or by agent			
Potential problems or disadvantages of this coverage			

Section J

Investments

The worksheets in this section are to be used with Chapters 13-17 of *Personal Finance*, Sixth Edition.

Web sites for Investment Information

Standard & Poors personal finance site	www.personalwealth.com
FinanCenter	www.financenter.com
Motley Fool	www.fool.com
CNN Financial News	www.cnnfn.com/index/html
Quicken	www.qfn.com
Bloomberg	www.bloomberg.com
Money Line	www.moneyline.com
Daily Rocket	www.dailyrocket.com
Basic investment information	www.investorama.com; www.invest-faq.com
National Assn. of Securities Dealers	www.investor.nasd.com
American Assn. of Individual Investors	www.aaii.org
Investment club information	www.better-investing.org
Securities & Exchange Commission	www.sec.gov/consumer/cyberfr.htm
Stock investment information	www.stockmaster.com; www.onr.com/stocks.html
Stock quotes & related data	www.wsrn.com; quote.yahoo.com; ww.quote.com
New York Stock Exchange	www.nyse.com
American Stock Exchange	www.amex.com
NASDAQ	www.nasdaq.com
Annual report information	www.zpub.com
Company information	www.hoovers.com
High-tech stock investing	www.techstocks.com; www.newshub.com
Bonds Online	www.bonds-online.com
T-Bill Direct	www.netfactory.com/mondenet/tbdira1.html
Savings bonds, treasury notes, and t-bonds	www.frbsf.org

Web sites for Investment Information continued

Emerging international markets information	www.bradynet.org
Morningstar	www.morningstar.net
Mutual Fund Education Alliance	www.networth.galt.com
Basic mutual fund information	www.networth.quicken.com/investments
	www.mfmag.com; www.bloomberg.com
No-load fund information	www.no-loadfunds.com/
Money-market fund information	www.moneyline.com/mic
Chicago Board of Trade	www.cbot.com
Chicago Mercantile Exchange	www.cme.com

Sheet 55 - Setting investment objectives

Purpose: To determine specific goals for an investment program.

Instructions: Based on short and long term objectives for your investment efforts, enter the items requested below.

For use with *Personal Finance* Sixth Ed., Kapoor, Dlabay & Hughes Page 410

Description of financial need	Amount	Date needed	Investment goal (safety, growth, income)	Level of risk (high, medium, low)	Possible investments to achieve this goal

Note: Sheets 58, 59, and 60 may be used to implement specific investment plans to achieve these goals.

Sheet 56 - Assessing risk for investments

Purpose: To assess the risk of various investments in relation to your personal risk tolerance and financial goals.

Instructions: List various investments you are considering based on the type and level of risk associated with each.

For use with
Personal Finance
Sixth Ed., Kapoor,
Dlabay & Hughes
Page 414

Level of risk	Loss of market value (market risk)	Type of risk Inflation risk	Interest rate risk	Liquidity risk
High risk				
Moderate risk				
Low risk				

Sheet 57 - Evaluating investment information

Purpose: To identify and assess useful investment information sources.

Instructions: Obtain samples of several investment information that you might consider to guide you in your investment decisions.

For use with *Personal Finance* Sixth Ed., Kapoor, Dlabay & Hughes Page 433

Criteria Evaluation	Item 1	Item 2	Item 3
Location (address, phone)			
Web site			
Overview of information provided (main features)			
Cost			
Ease of access			
Evaluation: • reliability • clarity • value of information compared to cost			

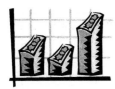

Sheet 58 – Using stocks to achieve financial goals

Purpose: To plan stock investments for specific financial goals.

Instructions: Use current and projected stock values and dividends to create an investment plan for achieving a goal.

For use with
Personal Finance
Sixth Ed., Kapoor,
Dlabay & Hughes
Page 460

Financial goal/amount _____

Stock

Date: _____

Company: _____

Purchase price per share: $ _____

Total cost including commission: $ _____

Value 1	**Value 2**	**Value 3**
Date: _____	Date: _____	Date: _____
Price per share: $ _____	Price per share: $ _____	Price per share: $ _____
Total value: $ _____	Total value: $ _____	Total value: $ _____

Financial goal/amount _____

Stock

Date: _____

Company: _____

Purchase price per share: $ _____

Total cost including commission: $ _____

Value 1	**Value 2**	**Value 3**
Date: _____	Date: _____	Date: _____
Price per share: $ _____	Price per share: $ _____	Price per share: $ _____
Total value: $ _____	Total value: $ _____	Total value: $ _____

Financial goal/amount _____

Stock

Date: _____

Company: _____

Purchase price per share: $ _____

Total cost including commission: $ _____

Value 1	**Value 2**	**Value 3**
Date: _____	Date: _____	Date: _____
Price per share: $ _____	Price per share: $ _____	Price per share: $ _____
Total value: $ _____	Total value: $ _____	Total value: $ _____

Note: Different stocks can be used for each financial goal, or a portfolio of several stocks can be used for a single financial goal.

Sheet 59 – Using bonds to achieve financial goals

Purpose: To plan bond investments to achieve specific financial goals.

Instructions: Use current and projected interest income and bond prices to create an investment plan for achieving a goal.

For use with
Personal Finance
Sixth Ed., Kapoor,
Dlabay & Hughes
Page 498

Financial goal/amount

Corporate Bond
Date: _____ Organization: _____ Purchase Price: $ _____
Type of bonds: _____
Interest rate annual amount _____%: $ _____
Total cost including commission: $ _____

Value 1	**Value 2**	**Value 3**
Date: _____	Date: _____	Date: _____
Price per bond: $ _____	Price per bond: $ _____	Price per bond: $ _____
Total value: $ _____	Total value: $ _____	Total value: $ _____
Interest earned: $ _____	Interest earned: $ _____	Interest earned: $ _____

Financial goal/amount

Corporate Bond
Date: _____ Organization: _____ Purchase Price: $ _____
Type of bonds: _____
Interest rate annual amount _____%: $ _____
Total cost including commission: $ _____

Value 1	**Value 2**	**Value 3**
Date: _____	Date: _____	Date: _____
Price per bond: $ _____	Price per bond: $ _____	Price per bond: $ _____
Total value: $ _____	Total value: $ _____	Total value: $ _____
Interest earned: $ _____	Interest earned: $ _____	Interest earned: $ _____

Financial goal/amount

Corporate Bond
Date: _____ Organization: _____ Purchase Price: $ _____
Type of bonds: _____
Interest rate annual amount _____%: $ _____
Total cost including commission: $ _____

Value 1	**Value 2**	**Value 3**
Date: _____	Date: _____	Date: _____
Price per bond: $ _____	Price per bond: $ _____	Price per bond: $ _____
Total value: $ _____	Total value: $ _____	Total value: $ _____
Interest earned: $ _____	Interest earned: $ _____	Interest earned: $ _____

Note: Different investments can be used for each financial goal, or a portfolio of several investments can be used for a single financial goal.

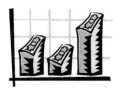

Sheet 60 – Using mutual funds and other investments

Purpose: To plan for using mutual funds and other investments to achieve specific financial goals.

Instructions: Use current and projected investment values and incomes to create an investment plan for achieving a goal.

For use with
Personal Finance
Sixth Ed., Kapoor,
Dlabay & Hughes
Page 538

Financial goal/amount _____

Mutual Fund

Date: _____ Company: _____

Type of fund: _____ Purchase price: $ _____

Number of shares: _____

Total cost including fees: $ _____

Value 1	**Value 2**	**Value 3**
Date: _____	Date: _____	Date: _____
NAV (net asset value): _____	NAV (net asset value): _____	NAV (net asset value): _____
$ _____	$ _____	$ _____
Total value: $ _____	Total value: $ _____	Total value: $ _____

Financial goal/amount _____

Mutual Fund

Date: _____ Company: _____

Type of fund: _____ Purchase price: $ _____

Number of shares: _____

Total cost including fees: $ _____

Value 1	**Value 2**	**Value 3**
Date: _____	Date: _____	Date: _____
NAV (net asset value): _____	NAV (net asset value): _____	NAV (net asset value): _____
$ _____	$ _____	$ _____
Total value: $ _____	Total value: $ _____	Total value: $ _____

Financial goal/amount _____

Mutual Fund

Date: _____ Company: _____

Type of fund: _____ Purchase price: $ _____

Number of shares: _____

Total cost including fees: $ _____

Value 1	**Value 2**	**Value 3**
Date: _____	Date: _____	Date: _____
NAV (net asset value): _____	NAV (net asset value): _____	NAV (net asset value): _____
$ _____	$ _____	$ _____
Total value: $ _____	Total value: $ _____	Total value: $ _____

Note: Different investments can be used for each financial goal, or a portfolio of several investments can be used for a single financial goal.

Sheet 61 – Investment broker comparison

Purpose: To compare the benefits and costs of different investment brokers.

Instructions: Compare the services of an investment broker based on the factors listed below.

For use with *Personal Finance* Sixth Ed., Kapoor, Dlabay & Hughes Chapter 17

Broker's name		
Organization		
Address		
Phone		
Web site		
Years of experience		
Education and training		
Areas of specialization		
Certifications held		
Professional affiliations		
Employer's stock exchange and financial market affiliations		
Information services offered		
Minimum commission charge		
Commission on 100 shares of stock at $50/share		
Fees for other investments: • corporate bonds • mutual funds • stock options		
Other fees: • annual account fee • inactivity fee • other		

Section K

Retirement & estate planning

The worksheets in this section are to be used with Chapters 18-19 of *Personal Finance*, Sixth Edition.

Web sites for Retirement and Estate Planning

Planning, assistance & articles	www.lifenet.com
	www.savingsnet.com
American Assn. of Retired Persons	www.aarp.org
Social Security Administration	www.ssa.gov
Roth IRA information	www.rothira.com
	www.pensionplanners.com
Pension plans	www.401K.com
	www.webcom.com/retire
American Express	www.americanexpress.com/401k
John Hancock Co.	www.jhancock.com
Fidelity Investments	www.personal.fidelity.com/retirement/toolkit.html
Estate planning information	www.webtrust.com
Wills & estate planning information	www.nolo.com
	www.mtpalermo.com
Federal estate tax information	www.irs.ustreas.gov
Estate taxes	www.lifenet.com/estate

Sheet 62 – Retirement housing and lifestyle planning

Purpose: To consider housing alternatives for retirement living, and to plan retirement activities.

Instructions: Evaluate current and expected needs and interest based on the items below.

For use with *Personal Finance* Sixth Ed., Kapoor, Dlabay & Hughes Chapter 18

Retirement housing plans

Description of current housing situation (size, facilities, location)

Time until retirement _____ years

Description of retirement housing needs

Checklist of retirement housing alternatives

_____ present home	_____ professional companionship arrangement
_____ house sharing	_____ commercial rental
_____ accessory apartment	_____ board and care home
_____ elder cottage hosing	_____ congregate housing
_____ rooming house	_____ continuing care retirement community
_____ single-room occupancy	_____ nursing home
_____ caretaker arrangement	

Personal and financial factors that will influence the retirement hosing decision

Financial planning actions to be taken related to retirement housing

Retirement activities

What plans do you have to work part-time or do volunteer work?

What recreational activities do you plan to continue or start?
(Location, training, equipment needs)

What plans do you have for travel or educational study?

Sheet 63 – Retirement plan comparison

Purpose: To compare benefits and costs for different retirement plans (401K, IRA, Keogh).

Instructions: Analyze advertisements and articles, and contact your employer and financial institutions to obtain the information below.

For use with *Personal Finance* Sixth Ed., Kapoor, Dlabay & Hughes Chapter 18

Type of plan			
Name of financial institution or employer			
Address			
Phone			
Web site			
Type of investments			
Minimum initial deposit			
Minimum additional deposits			
Employer contributions			
Current rate of return			
Service charges/fees			
Safety Insured? By whom?			
Amount			
Payroll deduction available			
Tax benefits			
Penalty for early withdrawal:			
IRS penalty (10%)			
other penalties			
Other features or restrictions			

Sheet 64 – Forecasting retirement income

Purpose: To determine the amount needed to save each year to have the necessary funds to cover retirement living costs.
Instructions: Estimate the information requested below.

For use with Personal Finance Sixth Ed., Kapoor, Dlabay & Hughes Chapter 18

Estimated annual retirement living expenses

Estimated annual living expenses
if you retired today $ _____

Future value for _____ years until
retirement at expected annual
income of _____ % (use future
value of $1, Exhibit A-1 of
Appendix A)   x _____

**Projected annual retirement living expenses
adjusted for inflation**... (A) $ _____

Estimated annual income at retirement

Social security income $ _____
Company pension, personal
retirement account income $ _____
Investment and other income $ _____

Total retirement income .... (B) $ _____

Additional retirement plan contributions (if B is less than A)

Annual shortfall of income after
retirement (A-B) $ _____

Expected annual rate of return on
invested funds after retirement,
percentage expressed as a
decimal $ _____

Needed investment fund after retirement A- B................. (C) $ _____

Future value factor of a series of deposits for _____ years until
retirement and an expected annual rate of return before
retirement of _____ % (Use Exhibit A-2 in Appendix A)   (D) $ _____

**Annual deposit to achieve needed investment fund (C
divided by D)**... $ _____

Sheet 65 – Estate planning activities

Purpose: To develop a plan for estate planning and related financial activities.

Instructions: Respond to the following questions as a basis for making and implementing an estate plan.

For use with
Personal Finance
Sixth Ed., Kapoor,
Dlabay & Hughes
Chapter 19

Are your financial records, including recent tax forms, insurance policies, and investment and housing documents, organized and easily accessible?	
Do you have a safe-deposit box? Where is it located? Where is the key?	
Location of life insurance policies. Name and address of insurance company and agent.	
Is your will current? Location of copies of your will. Name and address of your lawyer.	
Name and address of your executor	
Do you have a listing of the current value of assets owned and liabilities outstanding?	
Have any funeral and burial arrangements been made?	
Have you created any trusts? Name and location of financial institution.	
Do you have any current information on give and estate taxes?	
Have you prepared a letter of last instruction? Where is it located?	

Sheet 66 – Will planning sheet

Purpose: To compare costs and features of various types of wills.

Instructions: Obtain information for the various areas listed based on your current and future situation; contact attorneys regarding the cost of these wills

For use with
Personal Finance
Sixth Ed., Kapoor,
Dlabay & Hughes
Chapter 19

Type of will	Features that would be appropriate for my current or future situation	Cost Attorney, Address, Phone

Sheet 67 – Trust comparison sheet

Purpose: To identify features of different types of trusts.

Instructions: Research features of various trusts to determine their value to your personal situation.

For use with
Personal Finance
Sixth Ed., Kapoor,
Dlabay & Hughes
Chapter 19

Type of trust	Benefits	Possible value for my situation

Sheet 68 – Estate tax projection and settlement costs

Purpose: To estimate the estate tax based on your financial situation.

Instructions: Enter the data requested below to calculate the tax based on current tax rates.

For use with
Personal Finance
Sixth Ed., Kapoor,
Dlabay & Hughes
Chapter 19

Gross estate values

Personal property	$ _____	
Real estate	$ _____	
Joint ownership	$ _____	
Business interests	$ _____	
Life insurance	$ _____	
Employee benefits	$ _____	
Controlled gifts/trusts	$ _____	
Prior taxable gifts	$ _____	
Total estate values		$ _____

Deductible debts, costs, expenses

Mortgages and secured loans	$ _____	
Unsecured notes and loans	$ _____	
Bills and accounts payable	$ _____	
Funeral and medical expenses	$ _____	
Probate administration costs	$ _____	
Total deductions		-$ _____
Marital deduction		-$ _____
Taxable estate		=$ _____

Gross Estate Tax*
Allowable credits

Unified credit	$ _____	
Gift tax credit	$ _____	
State tax credit	$ _____	
Foreign tax credit	$ _____	
Prior tax credit	$ _____	
Total tax credits		-$ _____
Net Estate Tax		$ _____

*Consult the Internal Revenue Service for current rates and regulations related to estate taxes. (www.irs.gov)

Section L

Financial plan summary

The following worksheets are designed to summarize the actions needed to assess, plan, and achieve your personal financial goals:

Sheet 69   Financial data summary

Sheet 70   Savings/investment portfolio summary

Sheet 71   Progress check on major financial goals and activities

Sheet 72   Summary for money management, budgeting, and tax planning

Sheet 73   Summary for banking services and consumer credit

Sheet 74   Summary for consumer buying and housing

Sheet 75   Summary for insurance

Sheet 76   Summary for investments

Sheet 77   Summary for retirement and estate planning

As you complete the various sheets in the previous sections, transfer financial data, goals, and planned actions to the summary sheets in this section. For example:

Sheet	Actions to be taken	Planned completion date	Completed (√)
13 (financial documents & records)	locate and organize all personal financial documents	within 2-3 months	
19 (current income tax estimate)	sort current tax data, compute estimate to determine tax amount	February 15	√

Sheet 69 - Financial data summary

Date					
Balance sheet summary					
Assets					
Liabilities					
Net worth					
Cash flow summary					
Inflows					
Outflows					
Surplus/deficit					
Budget summary					
Budget					
Actual					
Variance					
Date					
Balance sheet summary					
Assets					
Liabilities					
Net worth					
Cash flow summary					
Inflows					
Outflows					
Surplus/deficit					
Budget summary					
Budget					
Actual					
Variance					

Sheet 70 – Savings/investment portfolio summary

Description	Organization contact/phone	Purchase price/date	Value/date	Value/date	Value/date	Value/date

Sheet 71 - Progress check on major financial goals and activities

Some financial planning activities require short-term perspective. Other activities may require continued efforts over a long period of time, such as purchasing a vacation home. This sheet is designed to help you monitor these long-term, ongoing financial activities.

Major financial objective	Desired completion date	Initial actions and date	Progress checks (date, progress made, and other actions to be taken)

Sheet 72 – Summary for money management, budgeting and tax planning activities
(Text Chapters 3-4)

Sheet	Actions to be taken	Planned completion date	Completed (√)

Sheet 73 – Summary for banking services and consumer credit activities

(Text Chapters 5-7)

Sheet	Actions to be taken	Planned completion date	Completed (√)

Sheet 74 – Summary for consumer buying and housing activities

(Text Chapters 8-9)

Sheet	Actions to be taken	Planned completion date	Completed (√)

Sheet 75 – Summary for insurance activities
(Text Chapters 10-12)

Sheet	Actions to be taken	Planned completion date	Completed (√)

Sheet 76 – Summary for investment activities
(Text Chapters 13-17)

Sheet	Actions to be taken	Planned completion date	Completed (√)

Sheet 77 – Summary for retirement and estate planning activities

(Text Chapters 18-19)

Sheet	Actions to be taken	Planned completion date	Completed (√)